DOODLE
MY WORLD

girls doodle book

By: Cristie Will

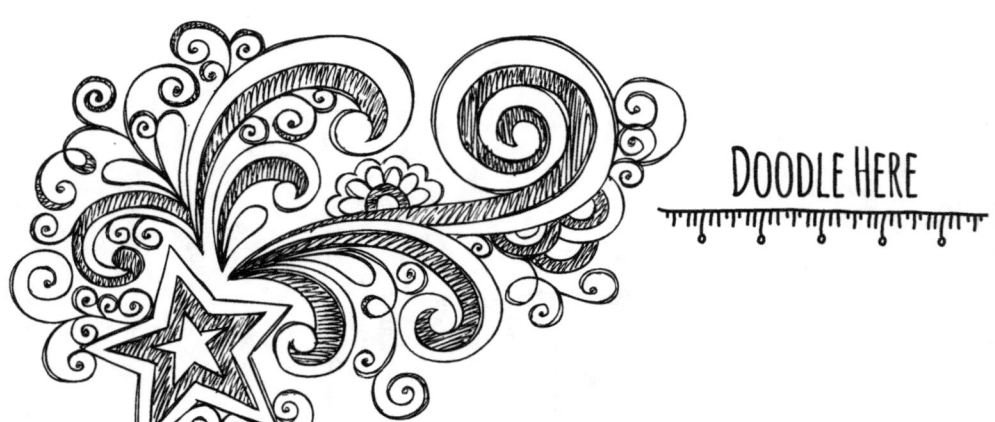

DOODLE HERE

DOODLE HERE

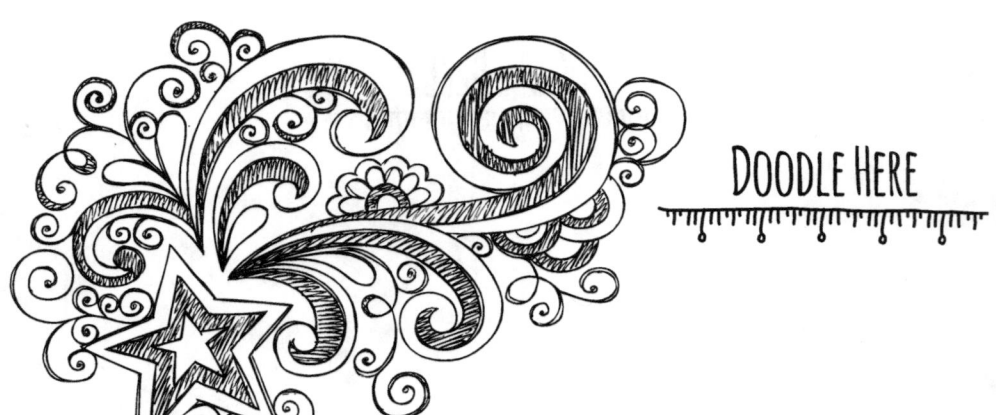

DOODLE HERE

DOODLE HERE

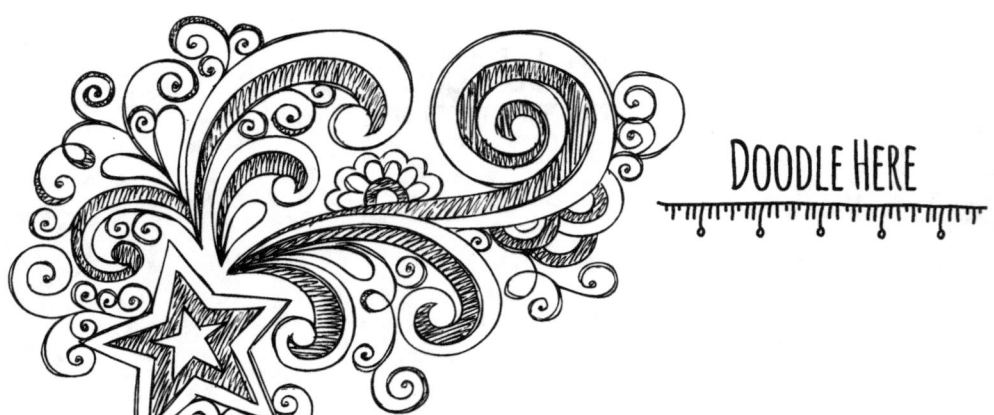

DOODLE HERE

DOODLE HERE

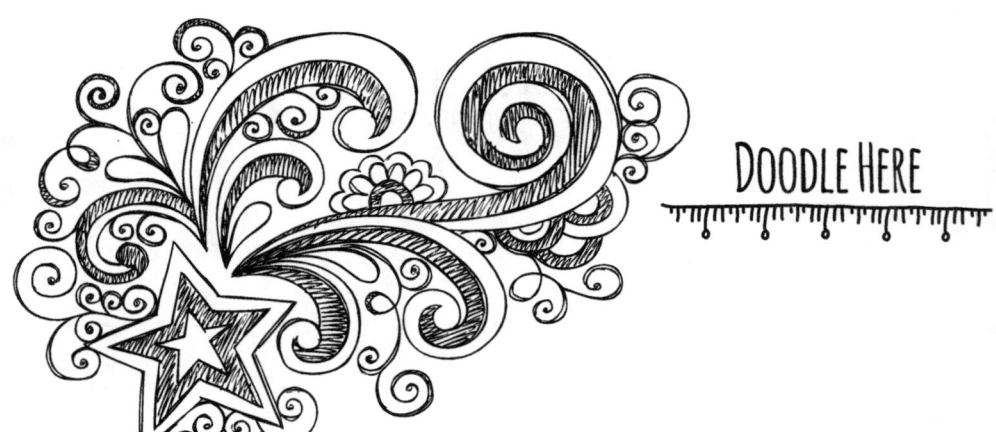

DOODLE HERE

DOODLE HERE

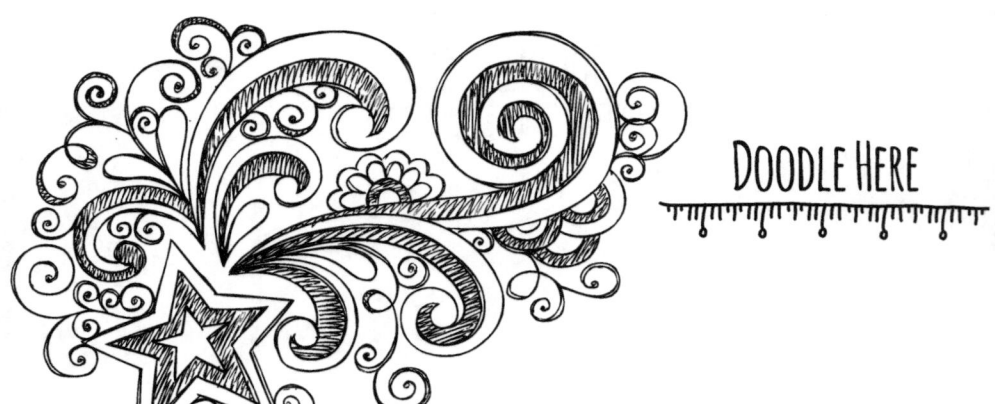

DOODLE HERE

DOODLE HERE

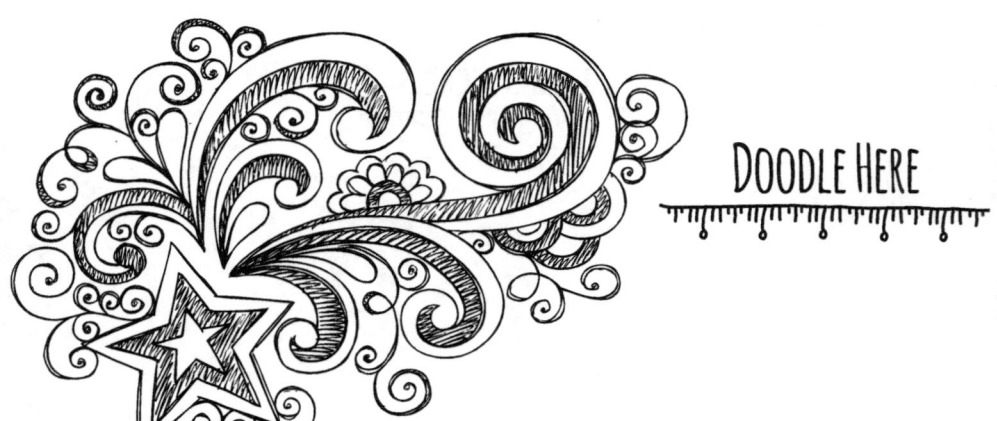

DOODLE HERE

DOODLE HERE

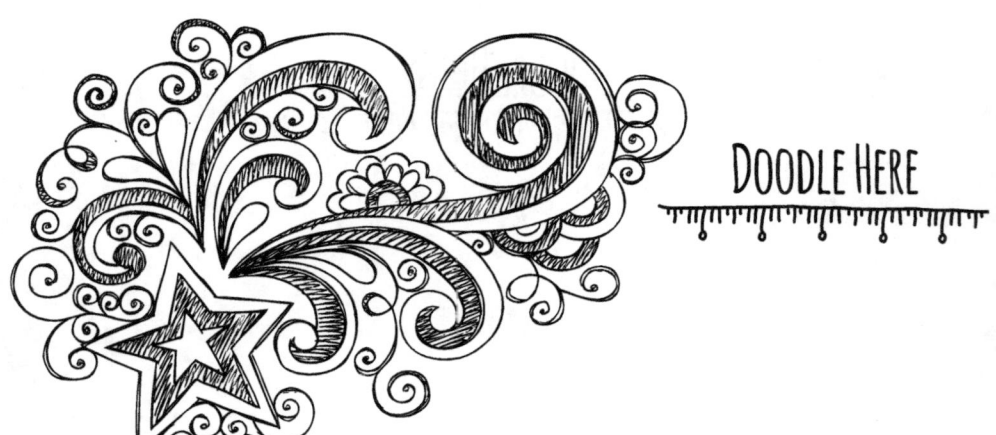

DOODLE HERE

DOODLE HERE

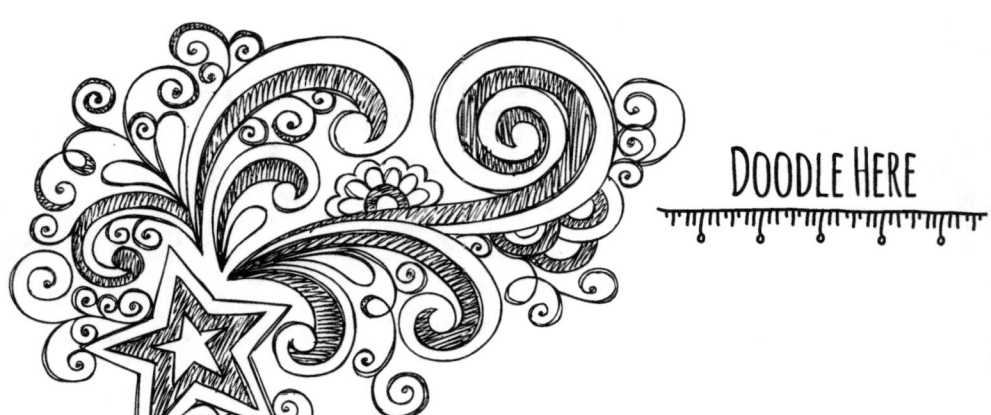

DOODLE HERE

DOODLE HERE

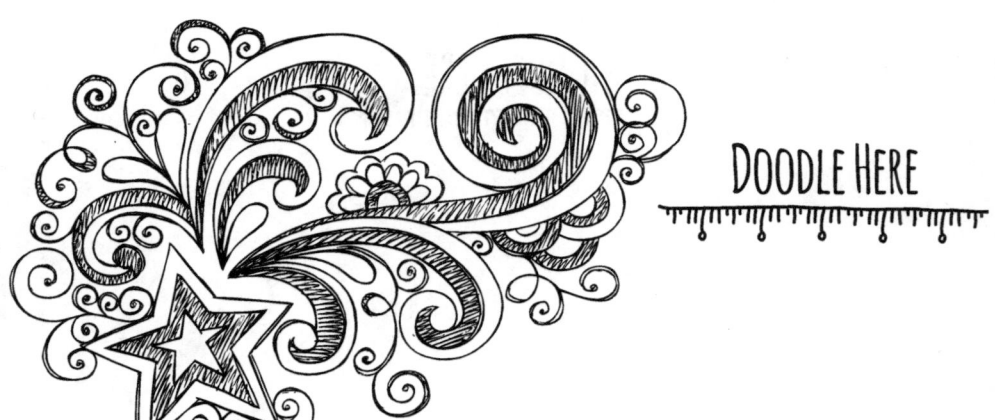

DOODLE HERE

DOODLE HERE

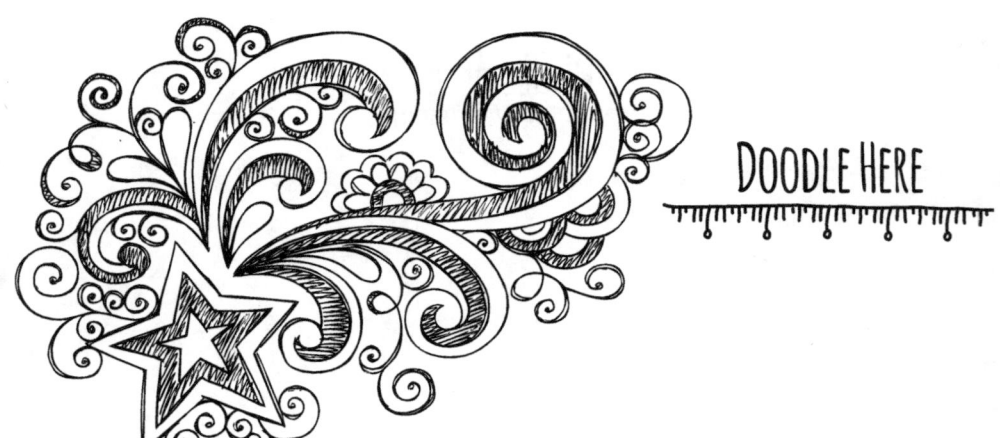

DOODLE HERE

DOODLE HERE

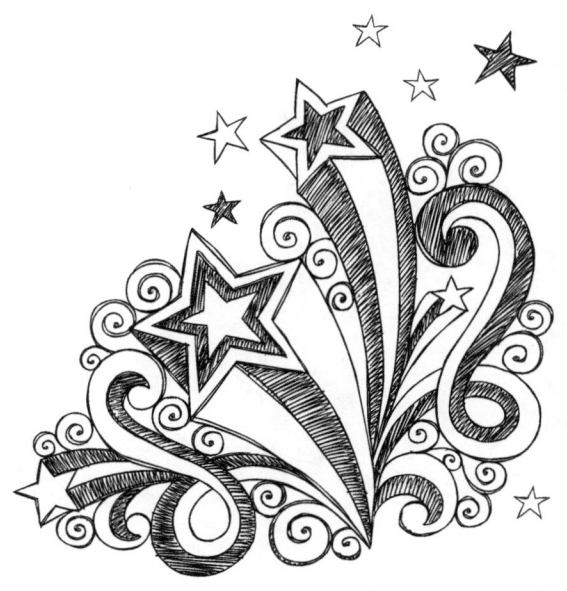

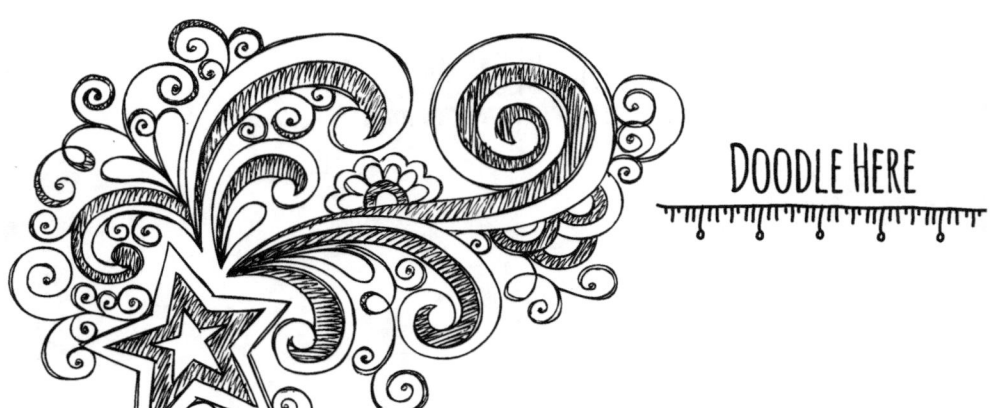

DOODLE HERE

DOODLE HERE

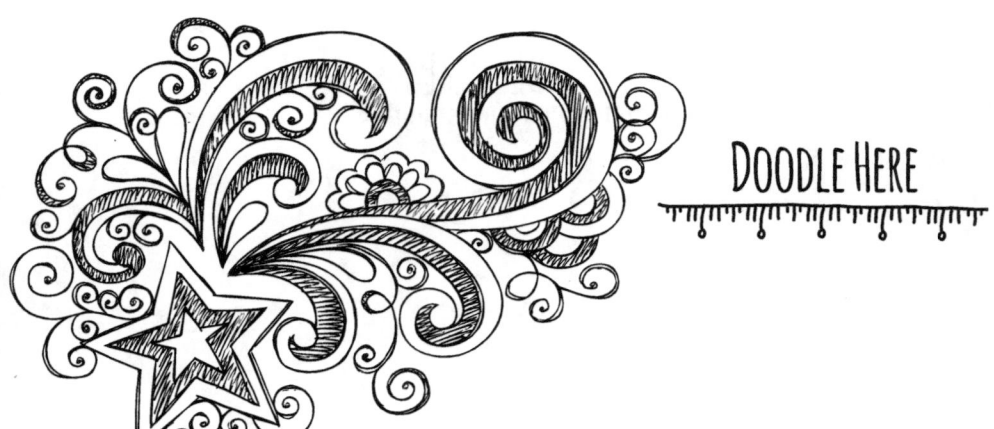

DOODLE HERE

DOODLE HERE

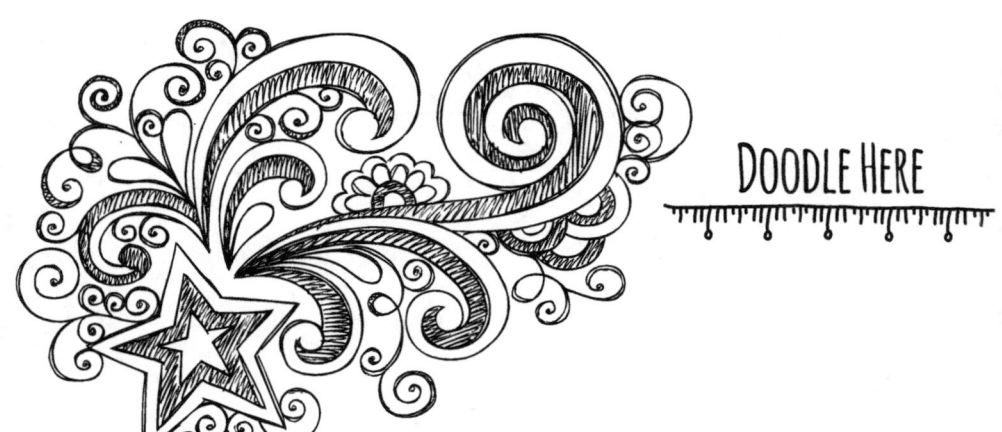

DOODLE HERE

DOODLE HERE

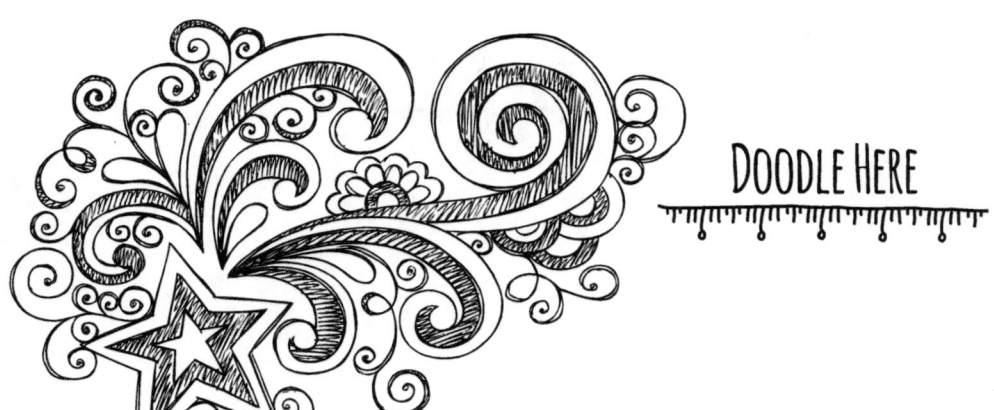

DOODLE HERE

DOODLE HERE

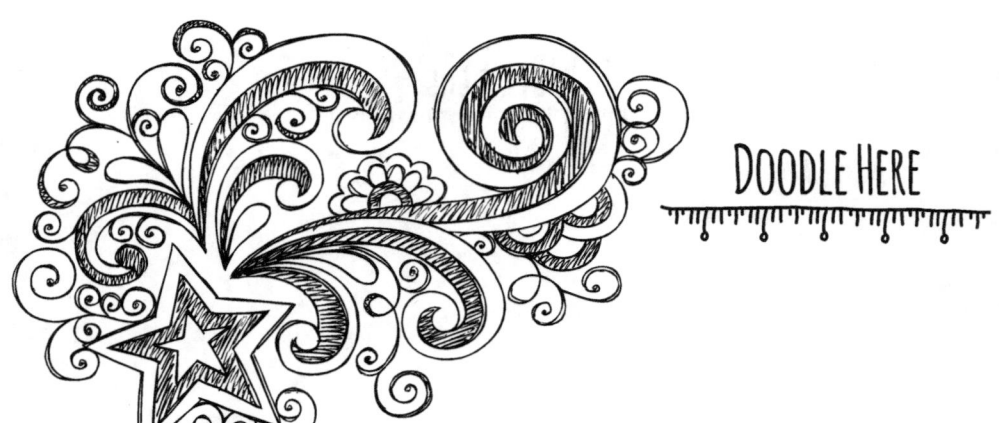

DOODLE HERE

DOODLE HERE

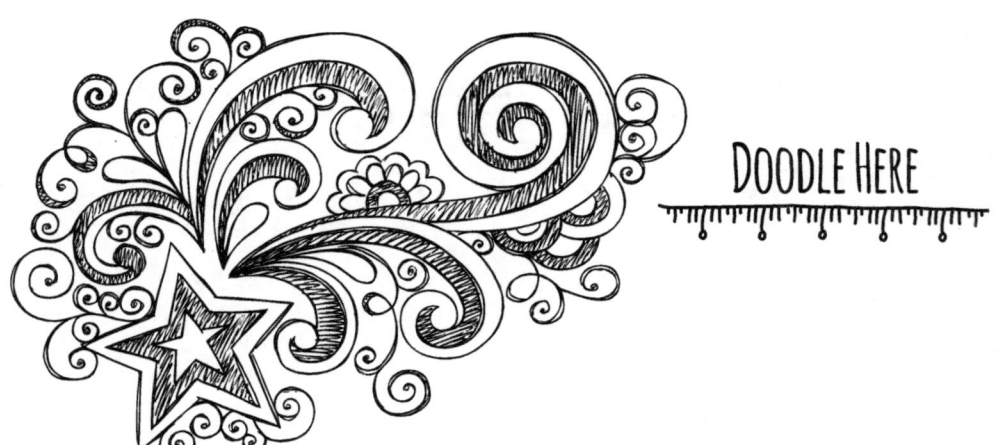

DOODLE HERE

DOODLE HERE

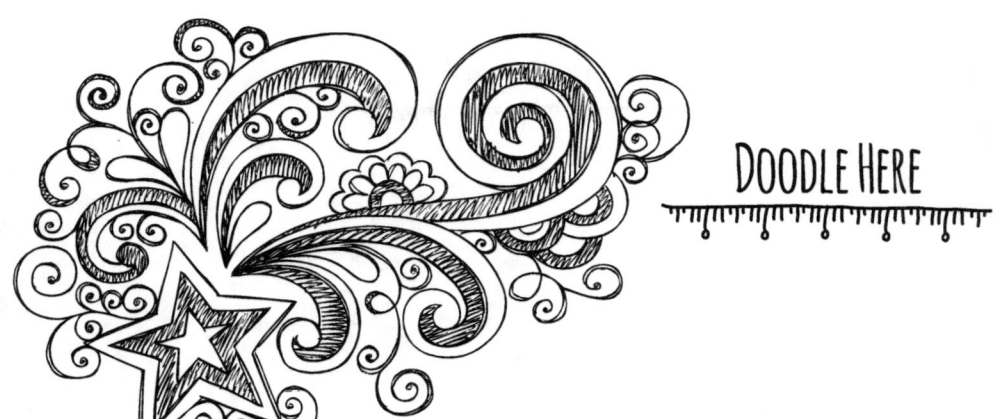

DOODLE HERE

DOODLE HERE

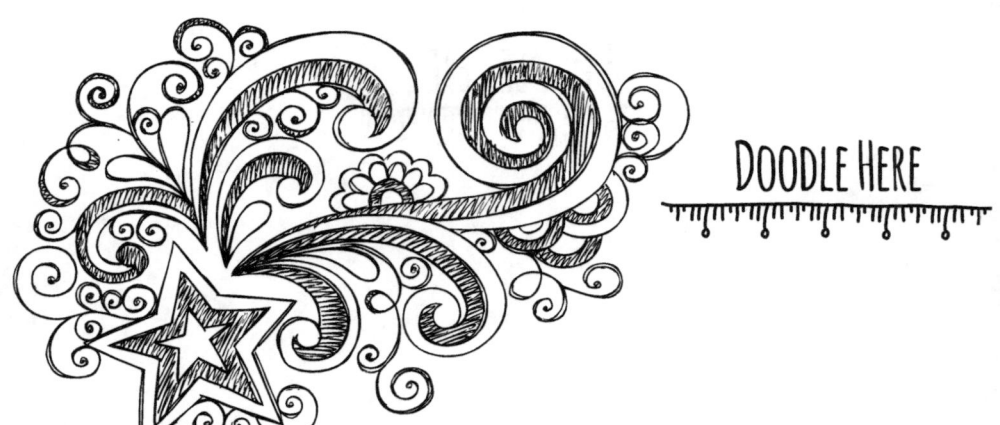

DOODLE HERE

DOODLE HERE

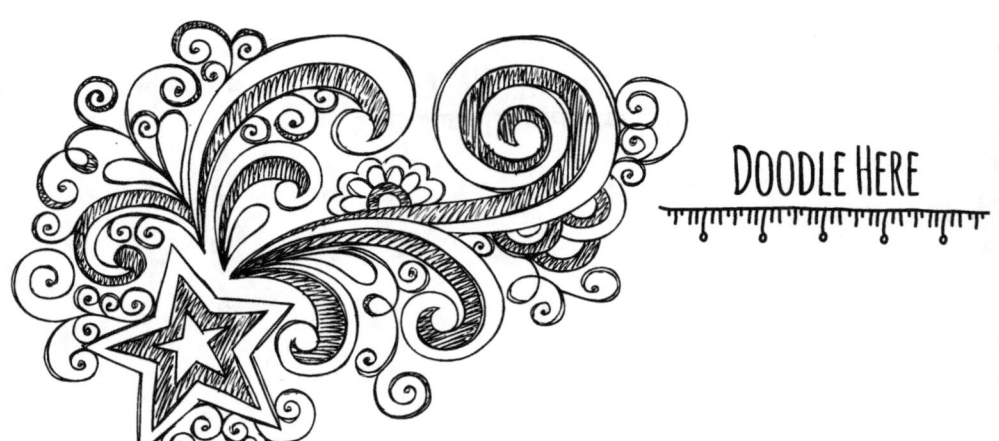

DOODLE HERE

DOODLE HERE

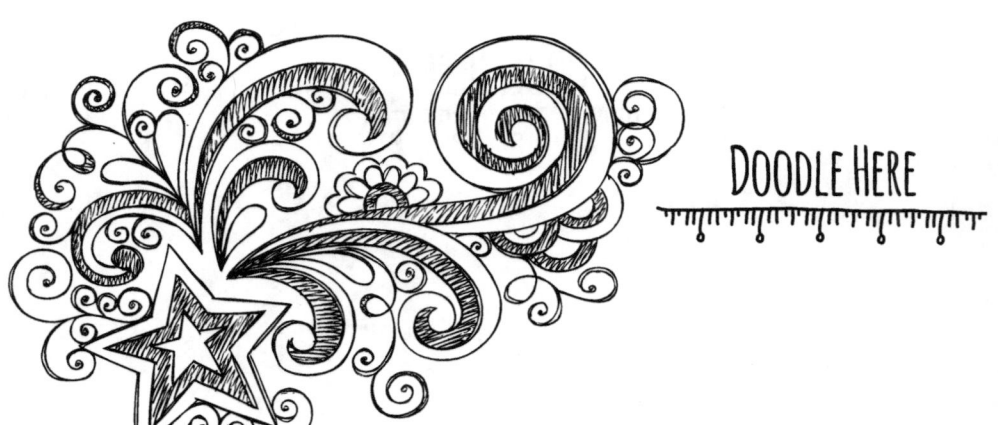

DOODLE HERE

DOODLE HERE

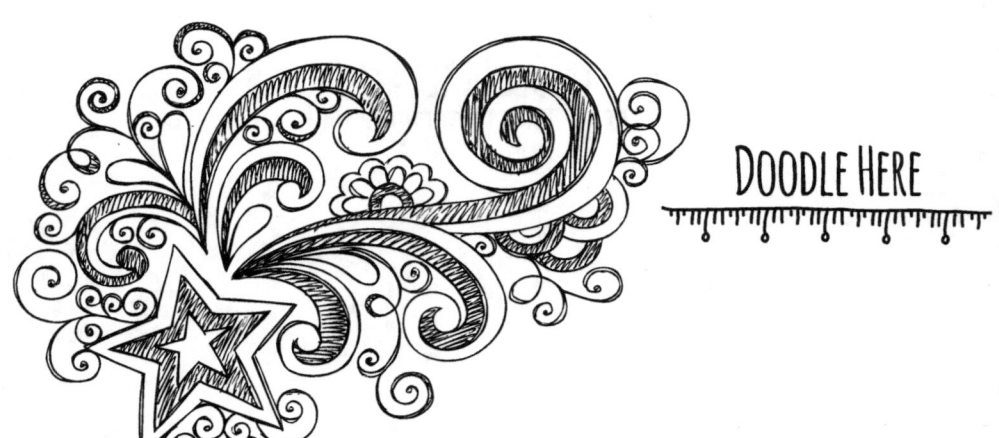

DOODLE HERE

DOODLE HERE

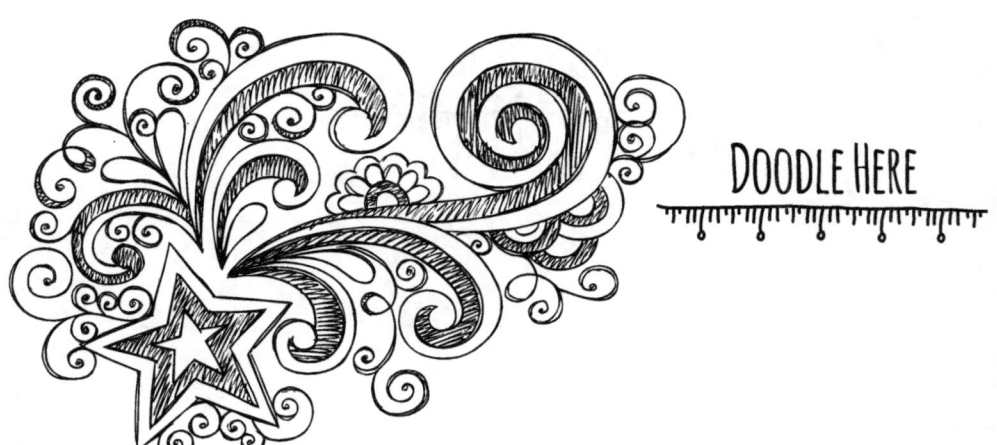

DOODLE HERE

DOODLE HERE

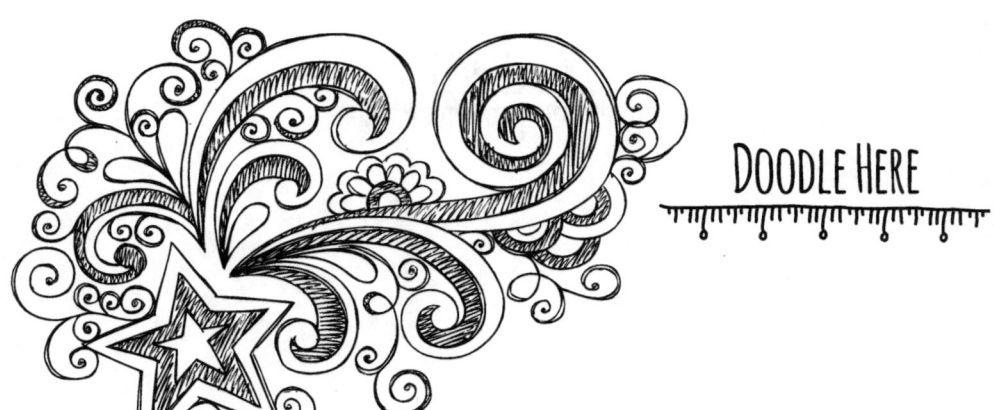

DOODLE HERE

DOODLE HERE

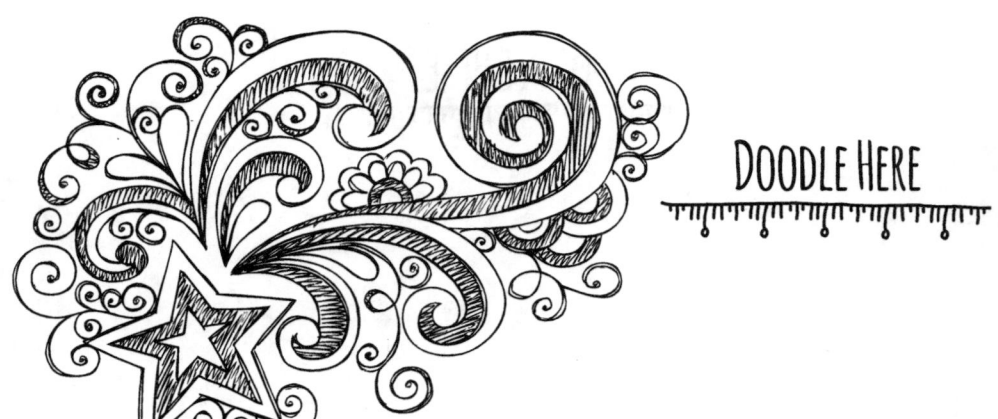

DOODLE HERE

DOODLE HERE

DOODLE HERE

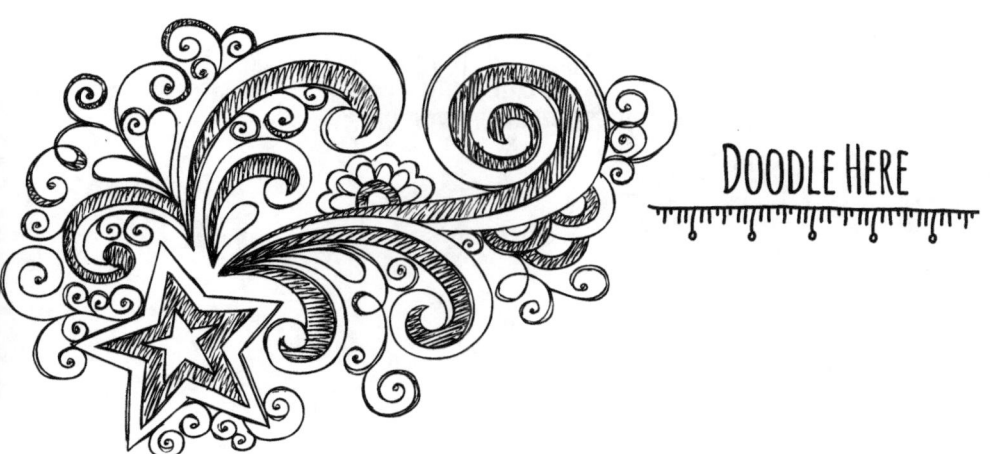

DOODLE HERE

DOODLE HERE

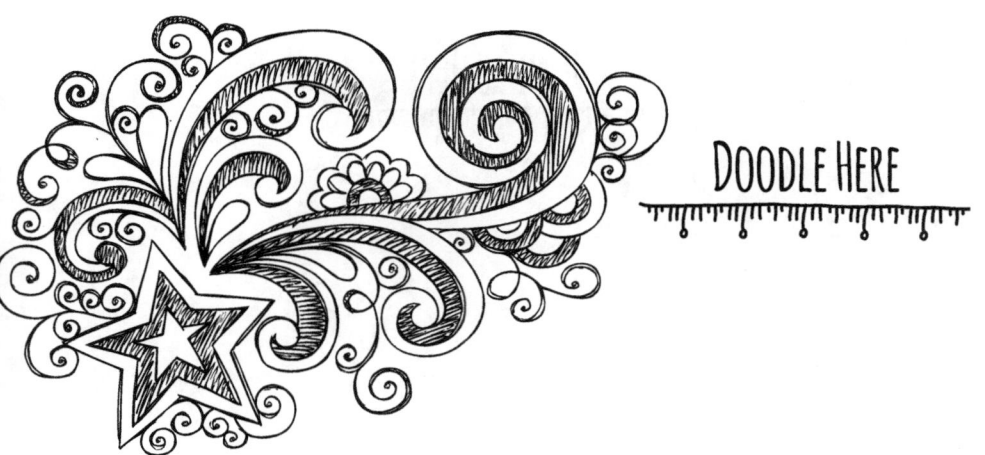

DOODLE HERE

DOODLE HERE

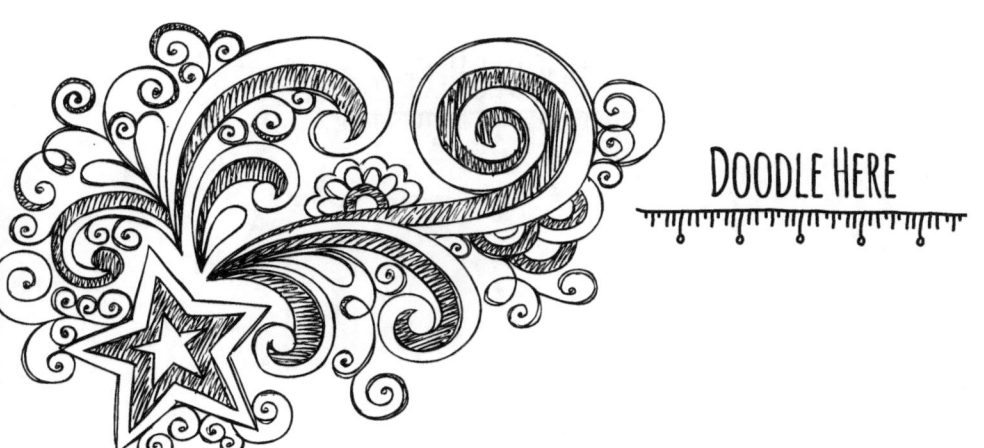

DOODLE HERE

DOODLE HERE

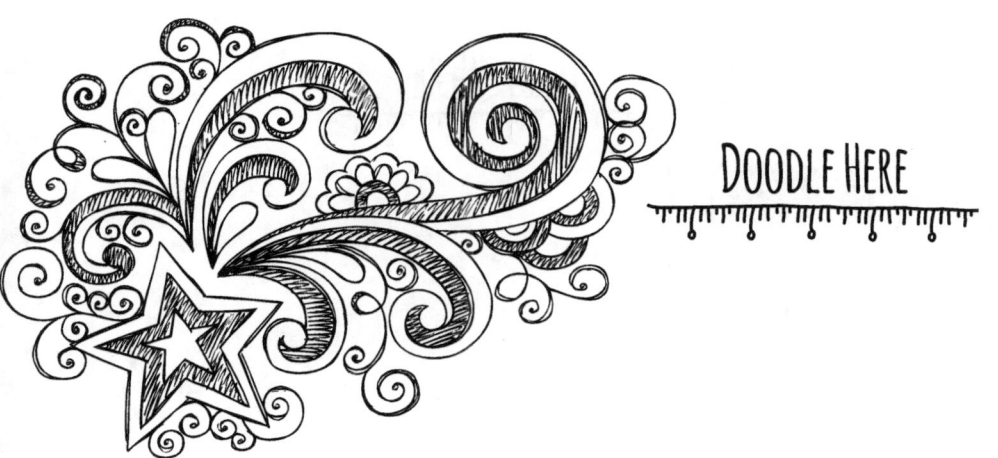

DOODLE HERE

DOODLE HERE

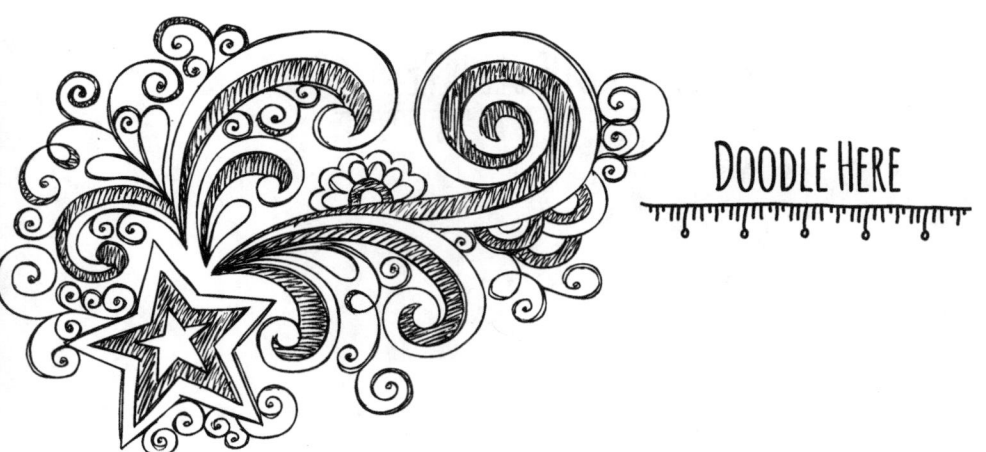

DOODLE HERE

DOODLE HERE

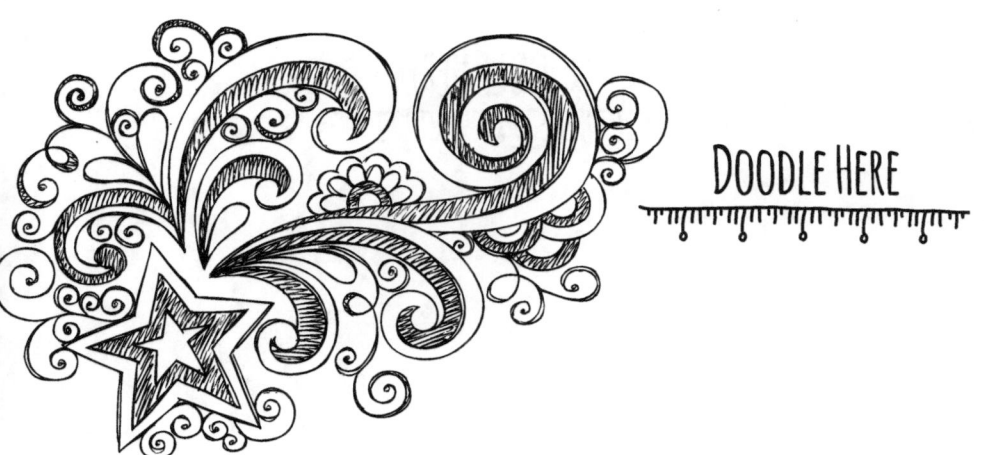

DOODLE HERE

DOODLE HERE

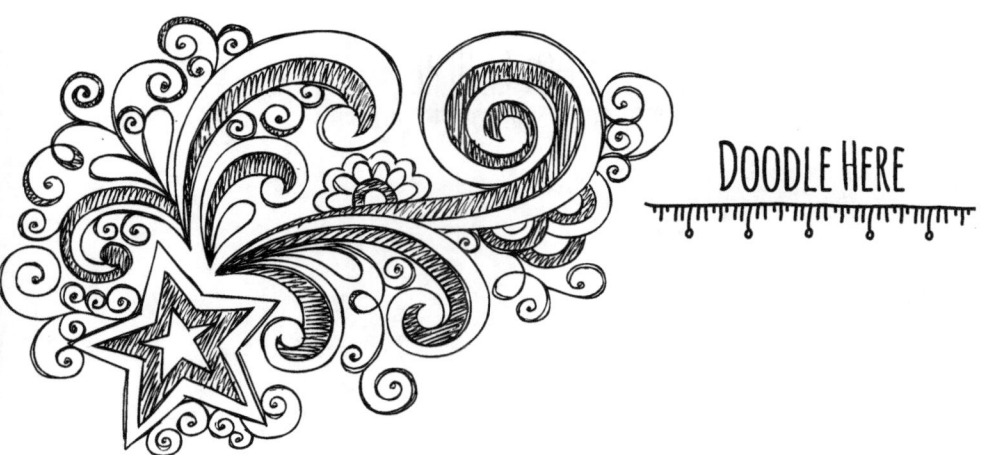

DOODLE HERE

DOODLE HERE

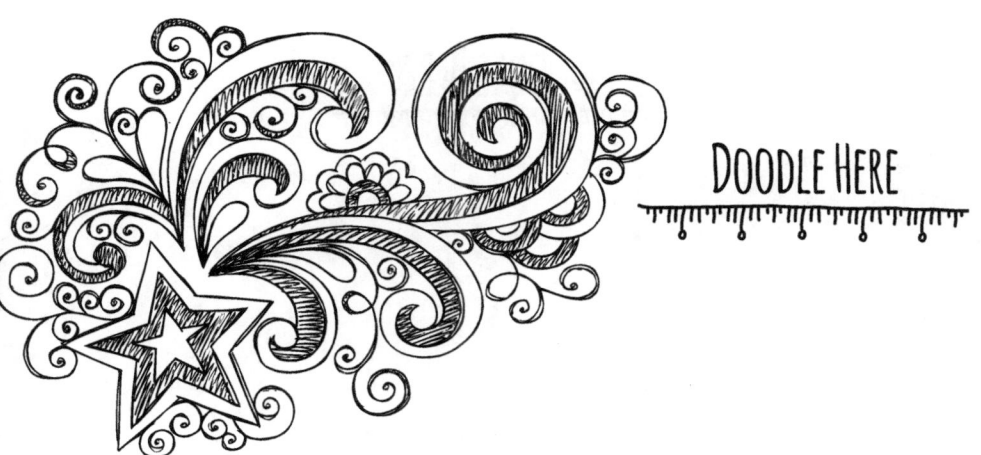

DOODLE HERE

DOODLE HERE

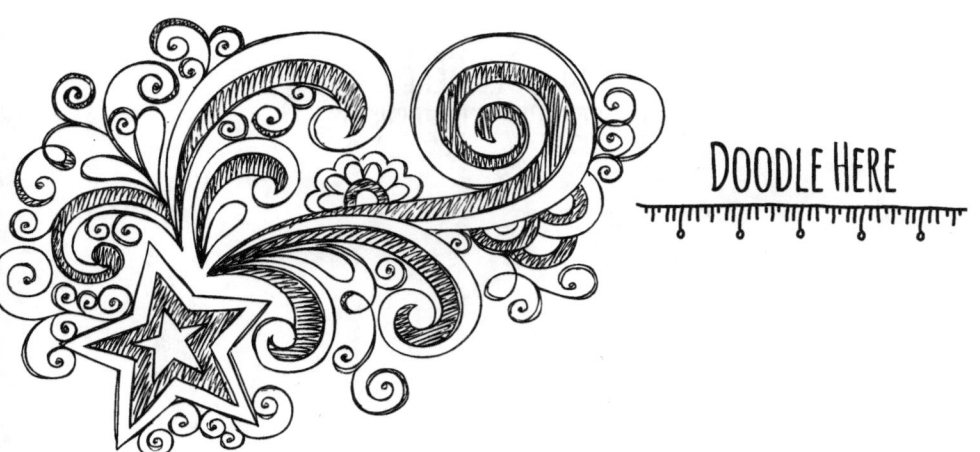

DOODLE HERE

DOODLE HERE

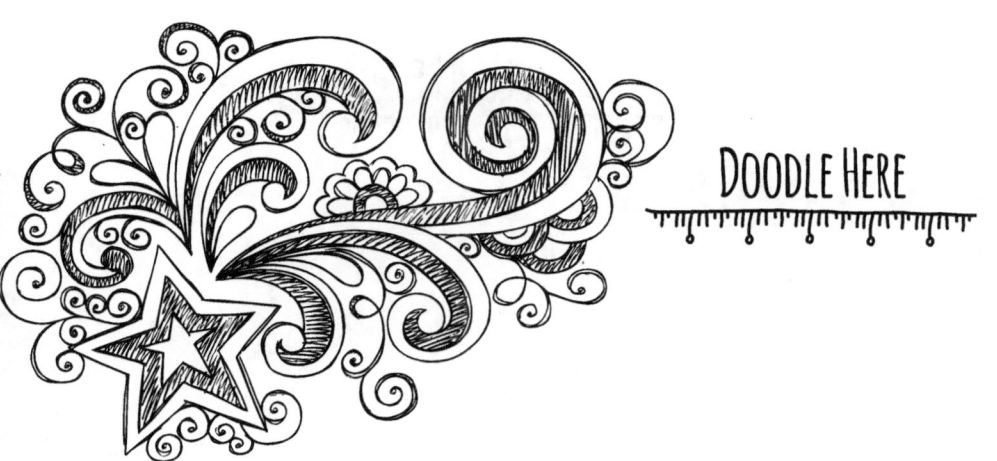

DOODLE HERE

DOODLE HERE

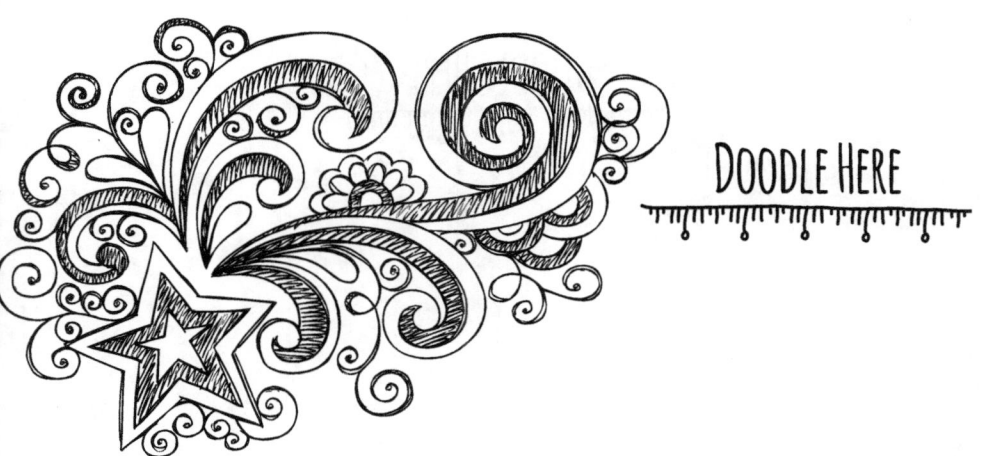

DOODLE HERE

DOODLE HERE

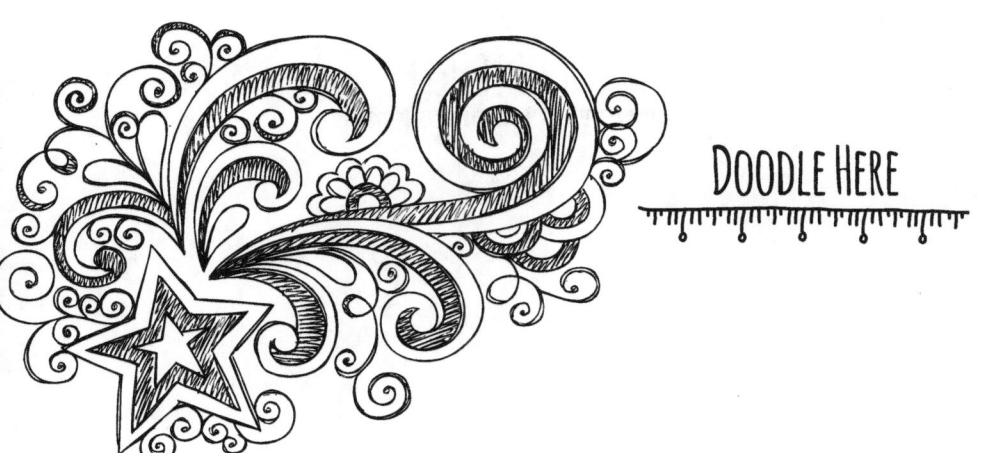

DOODLE HERE

DOODLE HERE

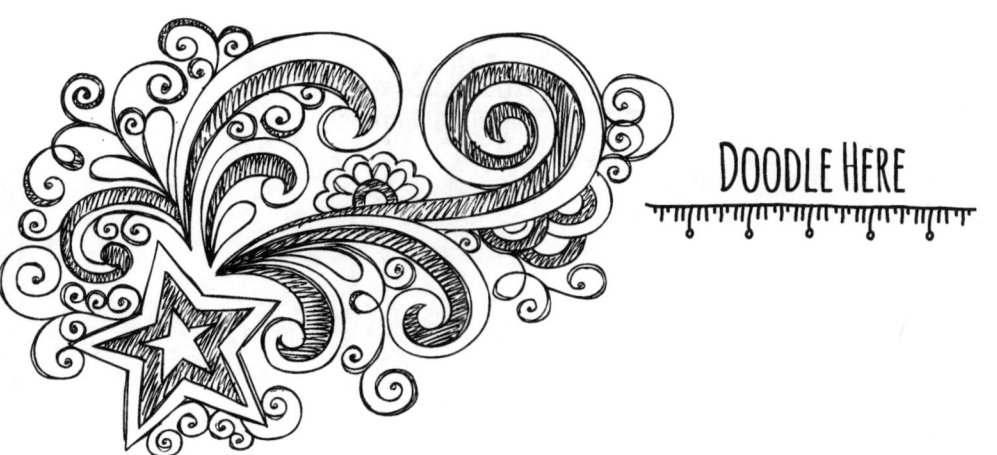

DOODLE HERE

DOODLE HERE

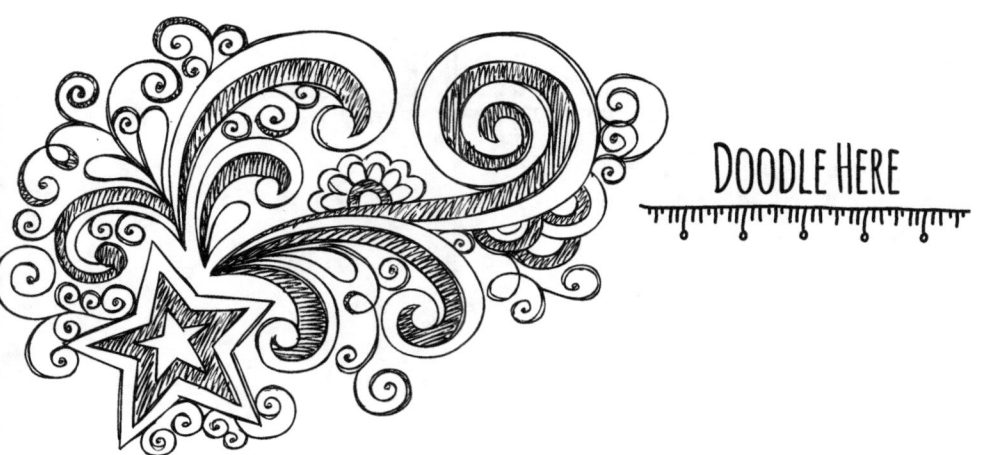

DOODLE HERE

DOODLE HERE

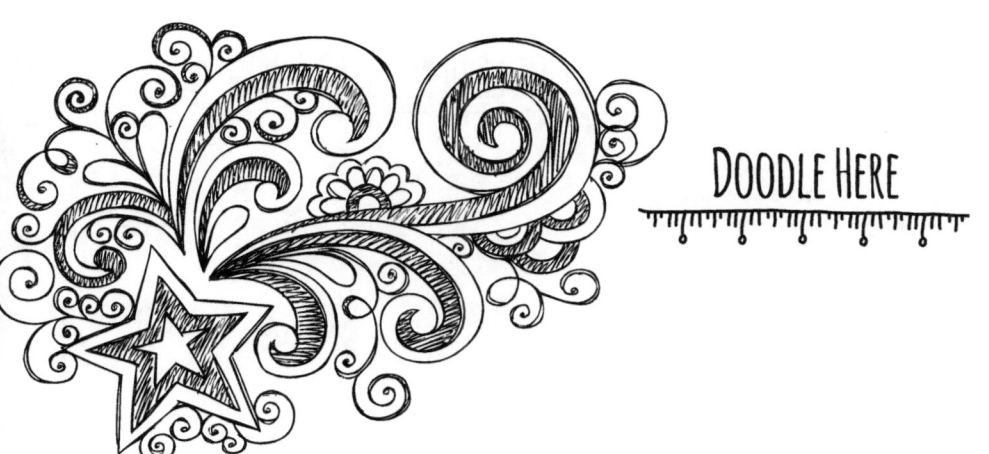

DOODLE HERE

DOODLE HERE

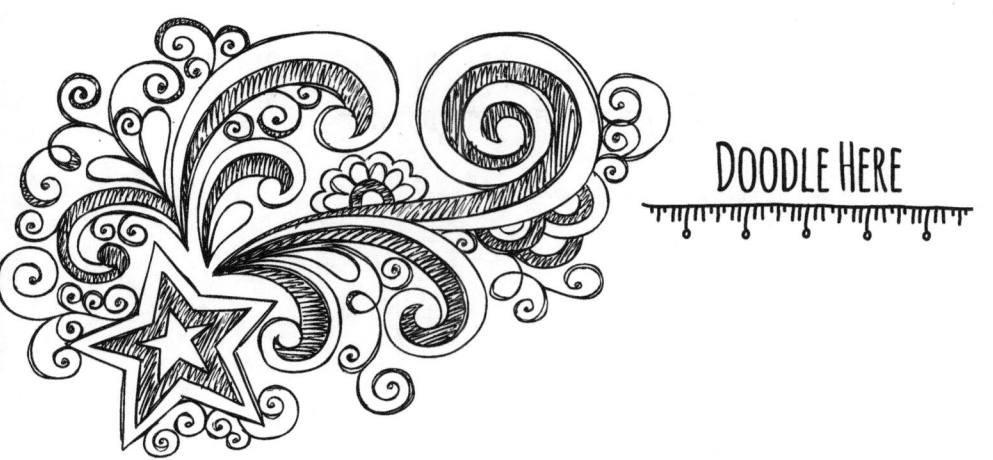

DOODLE HERE

DOODLE HERE

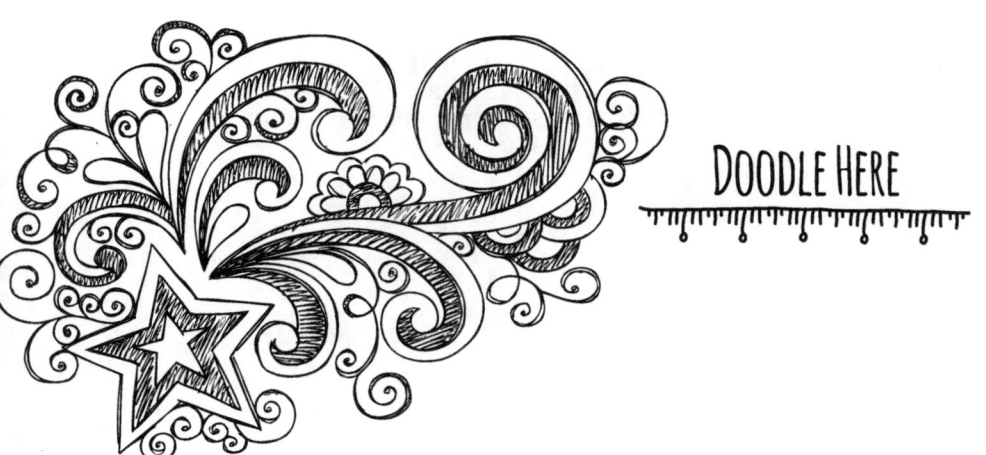

DOODLE HERE

DOODLE HERE

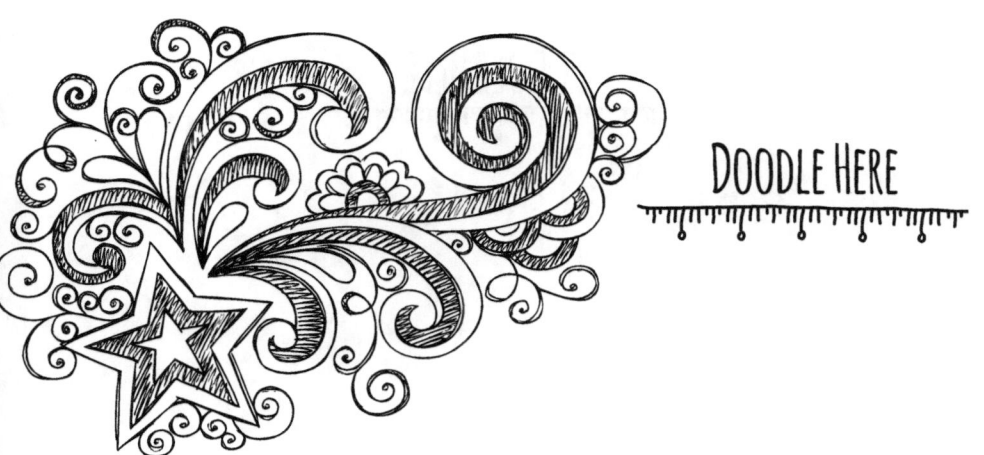

DOODLE HERE

DOODLE HERE

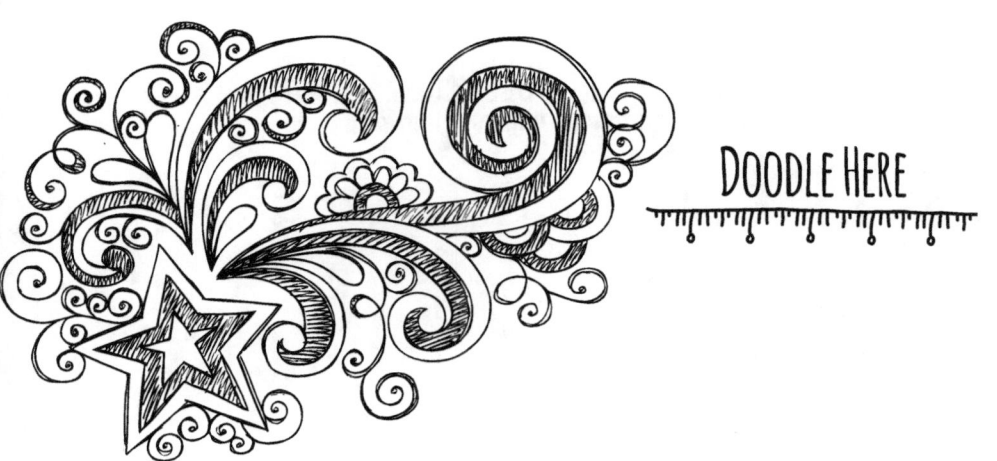

DOODLE HERE

DOODLE HERE

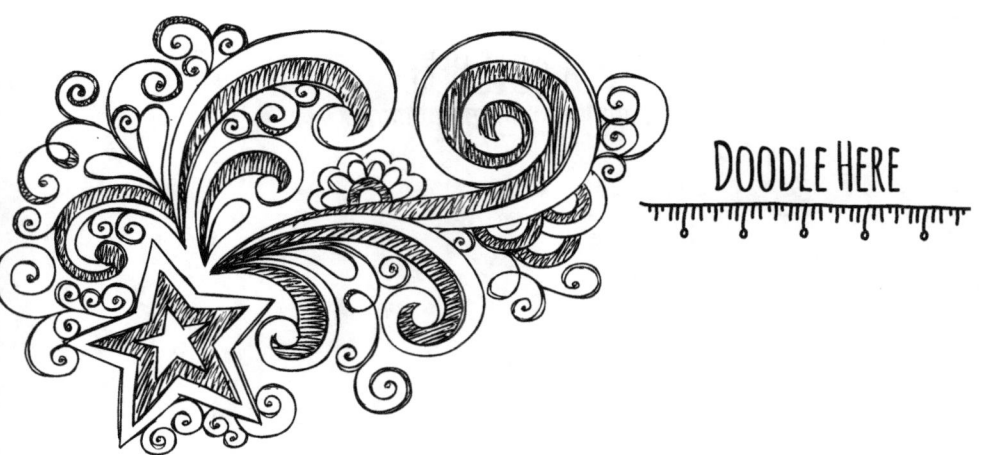

DOODLE HERE

DOODLE HERE

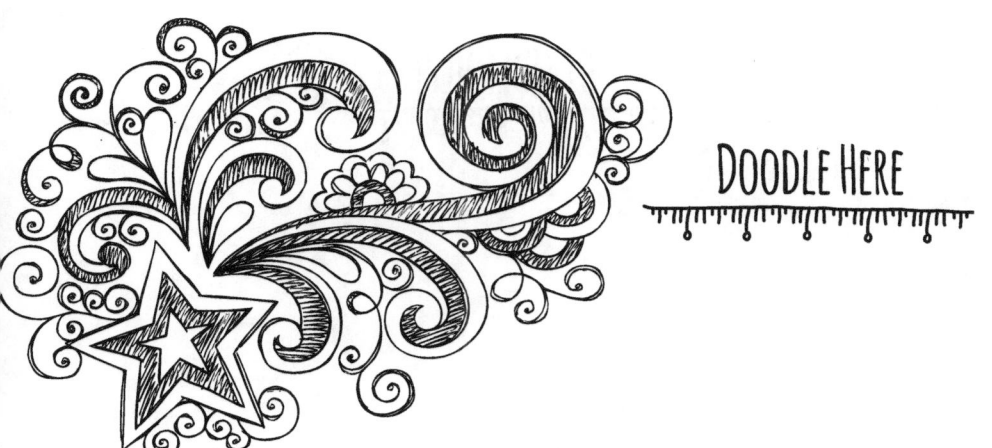

DOODLE HERE

DOODLE HERE

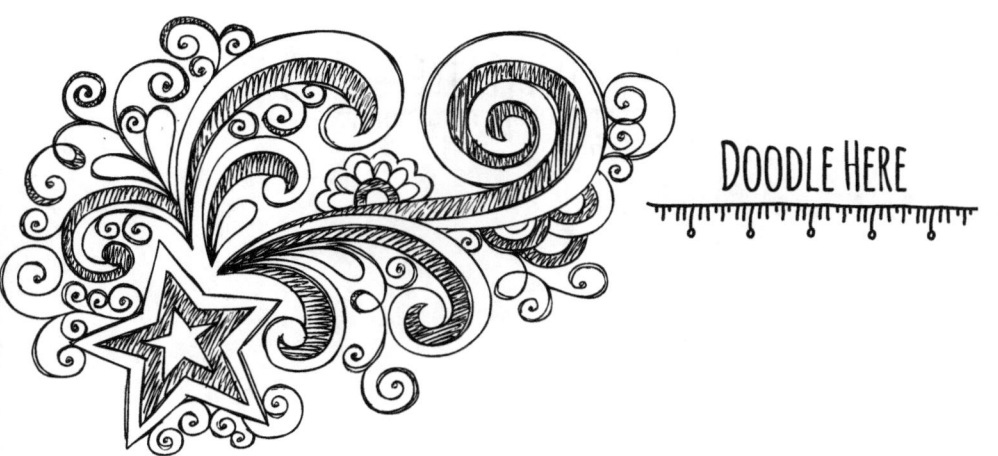

DOODLE HERE

DOODLE HERE

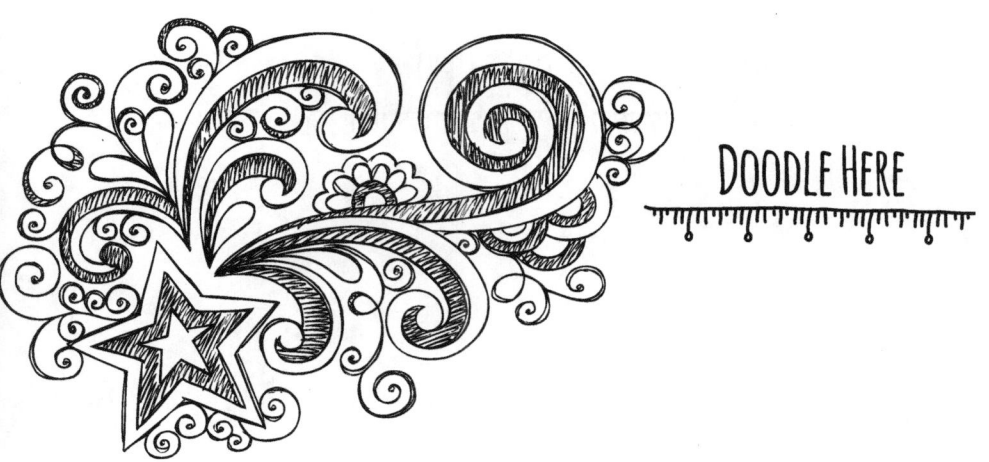

DOODLE HERE

DOODLE HERE

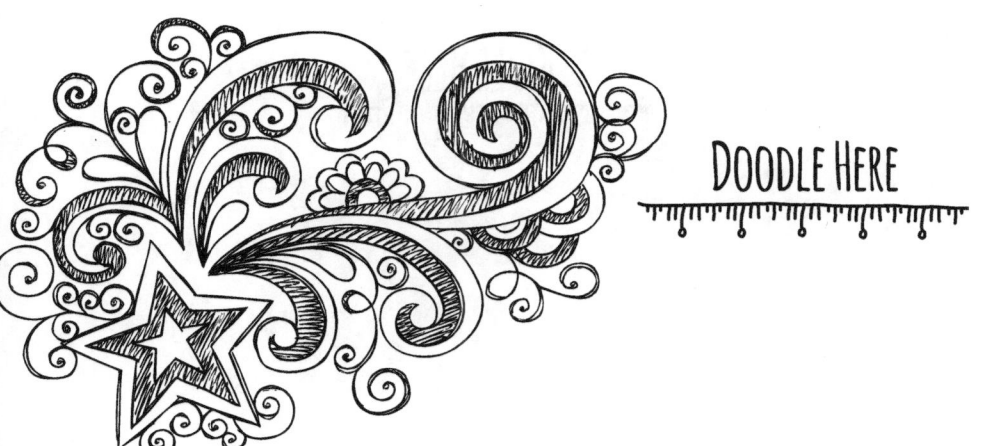

DOODLE HERE

DOODLE HERE

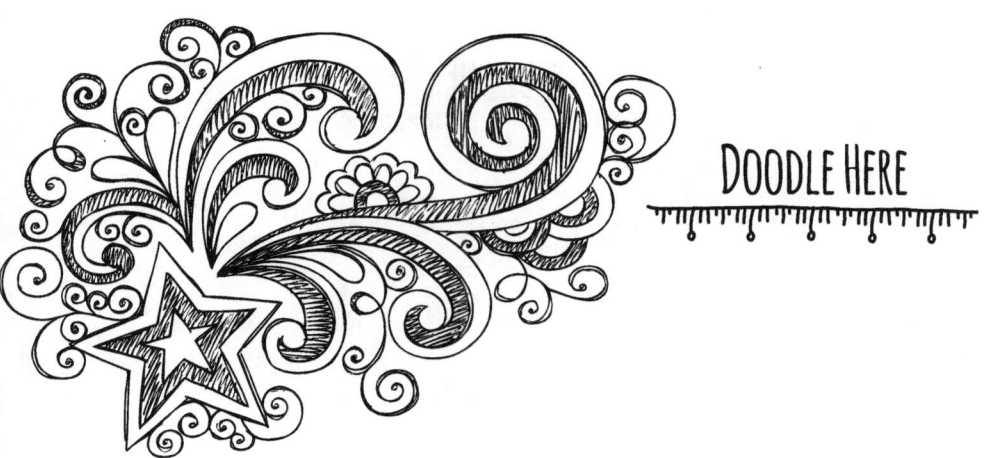

DOODLE HERE

DOODLE HERE

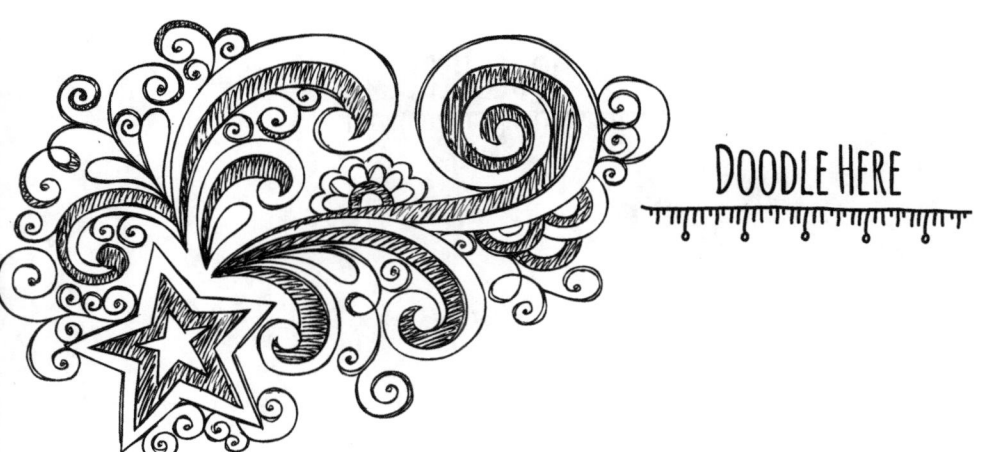

DOODLE HERE

DOODLE HERE

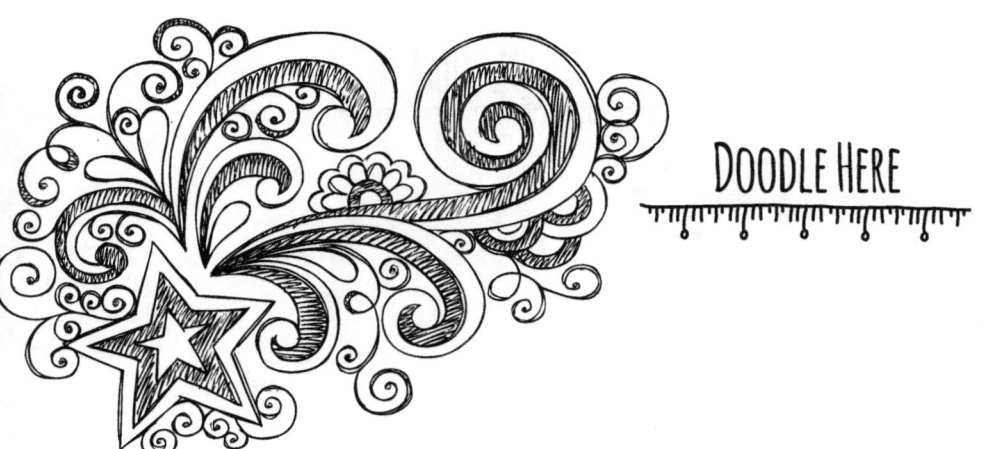

DOODLE HERE

DOODLE HERE

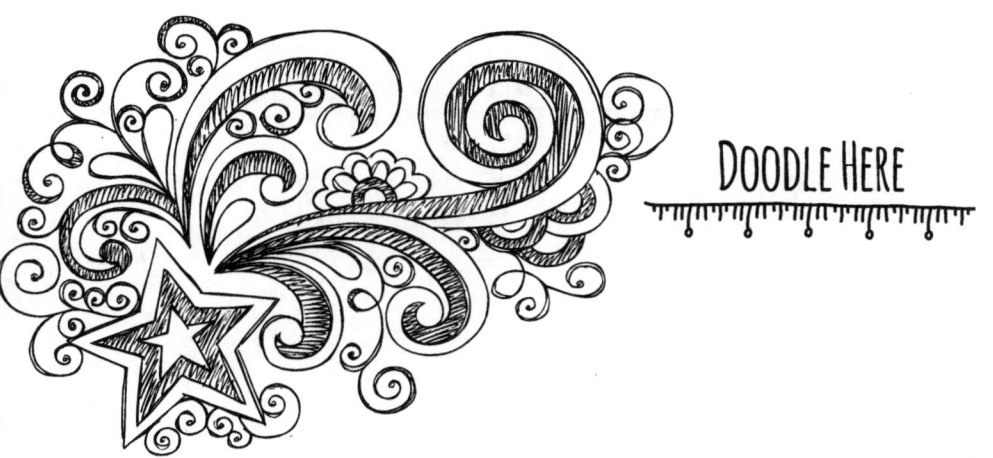

DOODLE HERE

DOODLE HERE

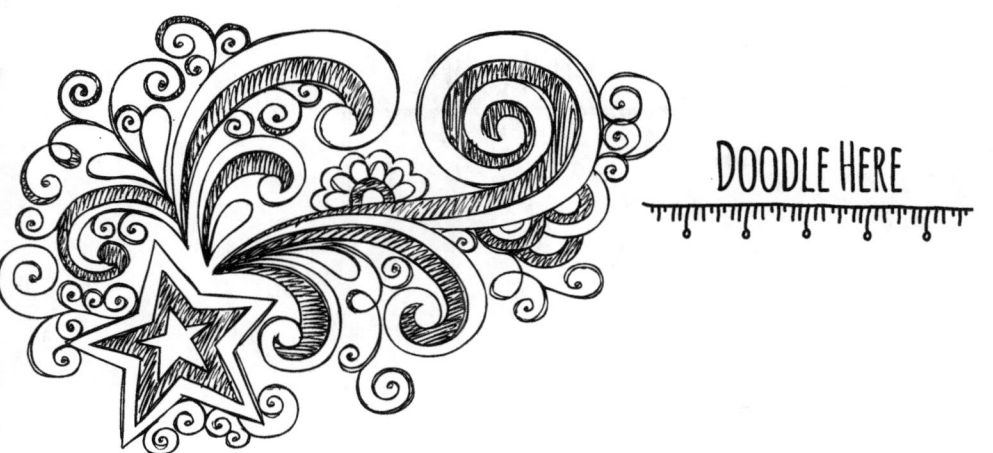

DOODLE HERE

DOODLE HERE

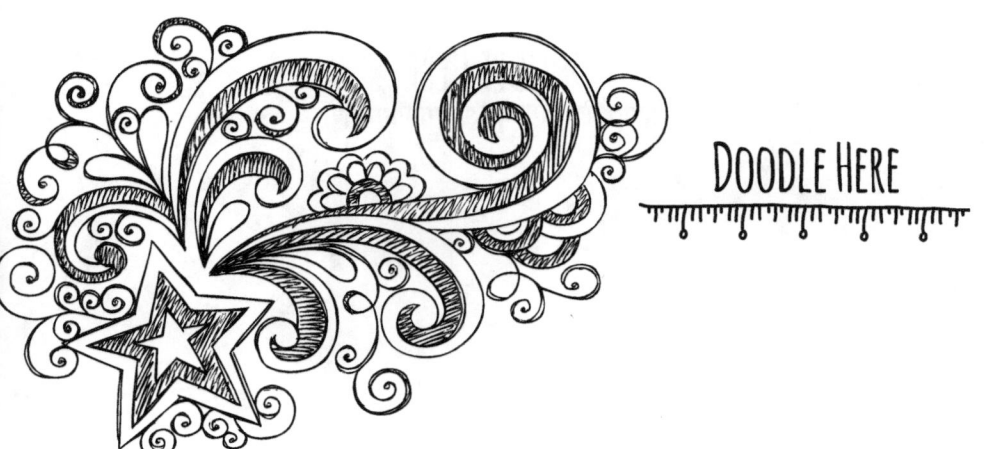

DOODLE HERE

DOODLE HERE

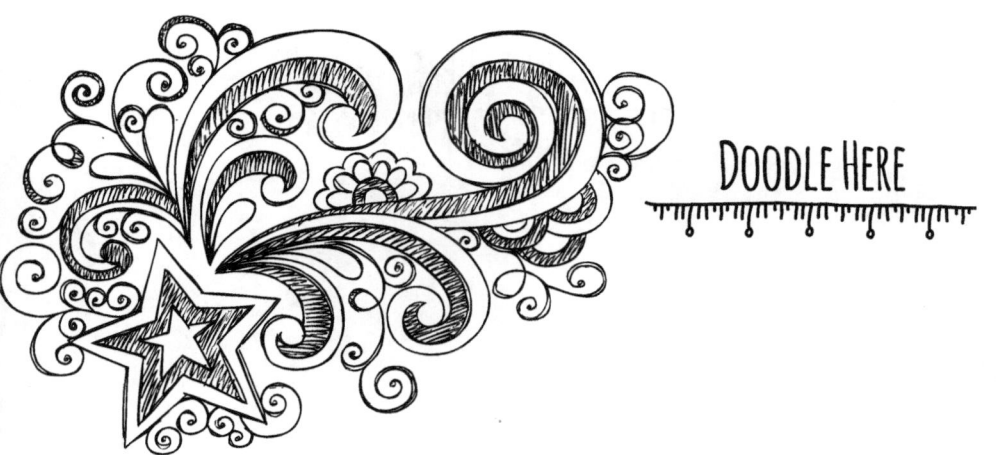

DOODLE HERE

DOODLE HERE

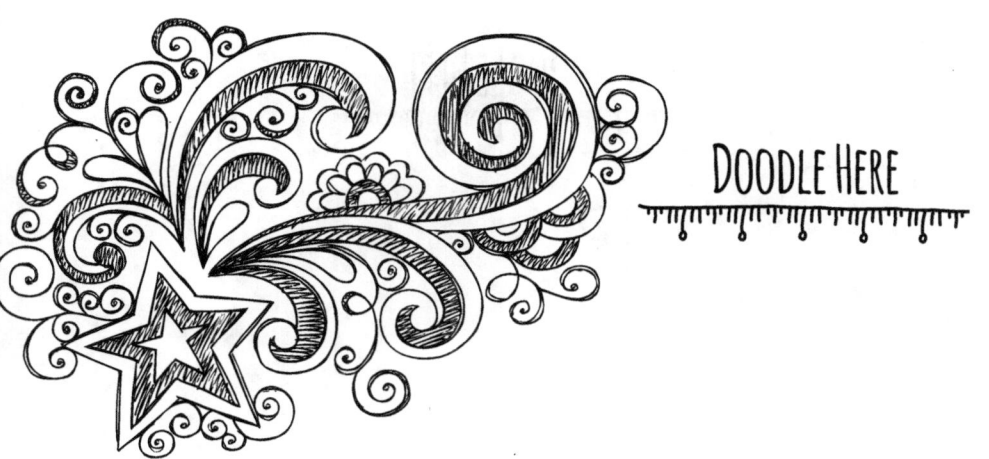

DOODLE HERE

DOODLE HERE

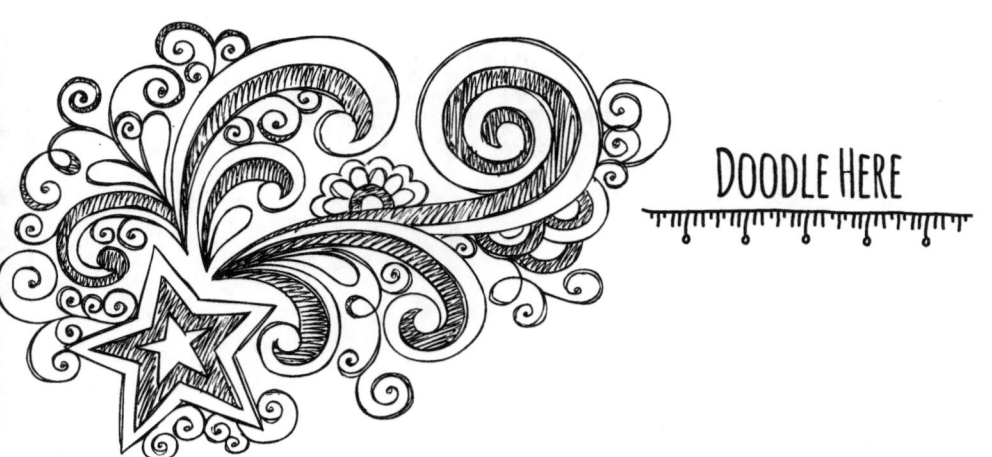

DOODLE HERE

DOODLE HERE

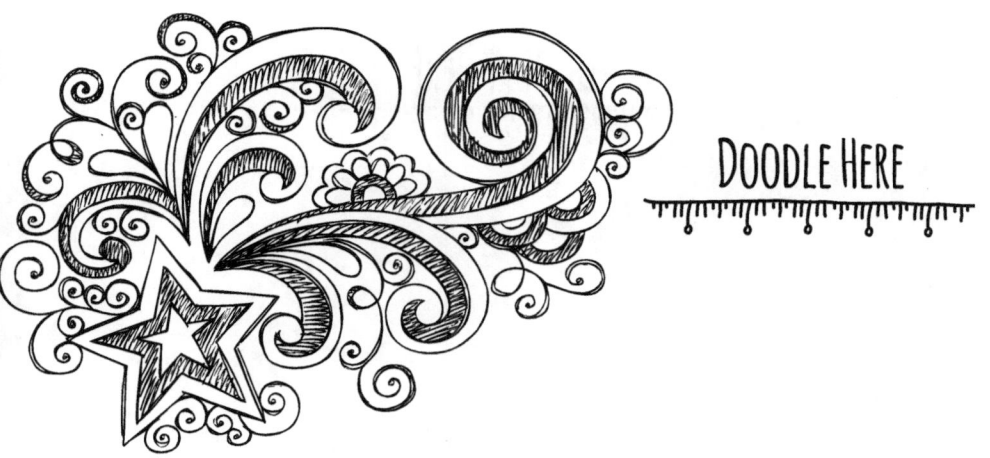

DOODLE HERE

DOODLE HERE

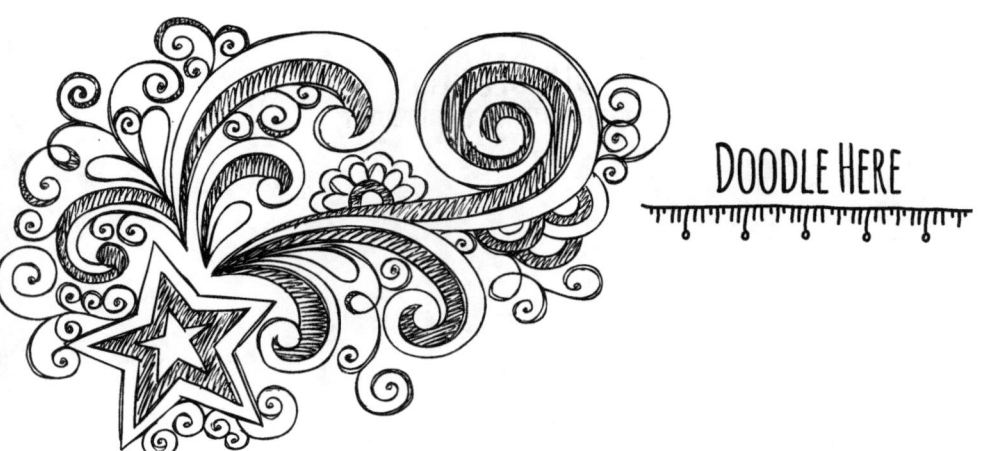

DOODLE HERE

DOODLE HERE

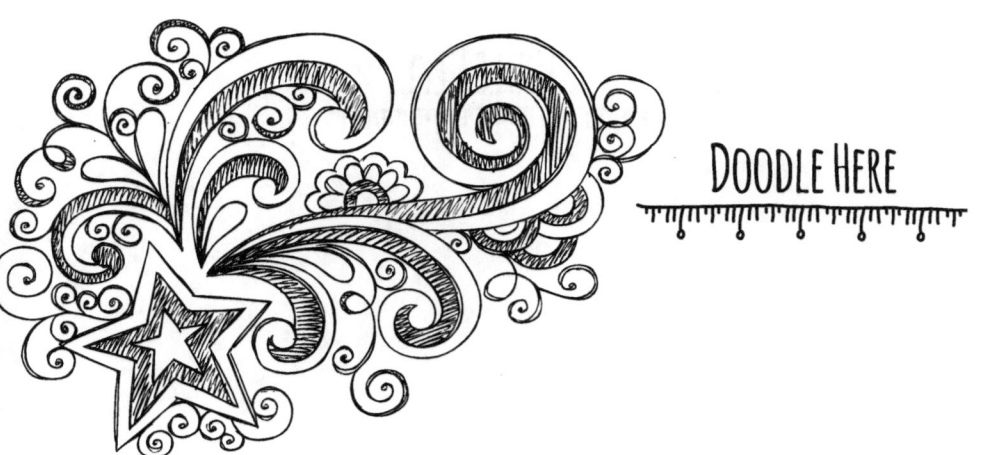

DOODLE HERE

DOODLE HERE

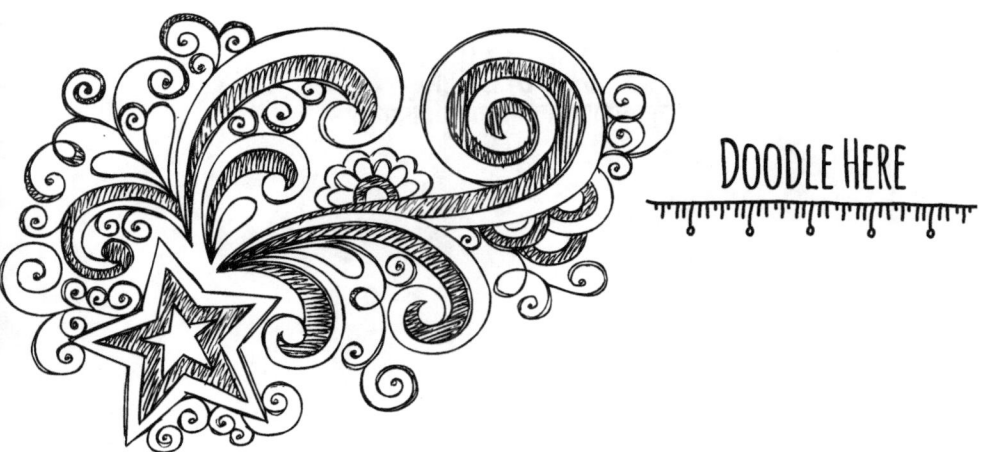

DOODLE HERE

DOODLE HERE

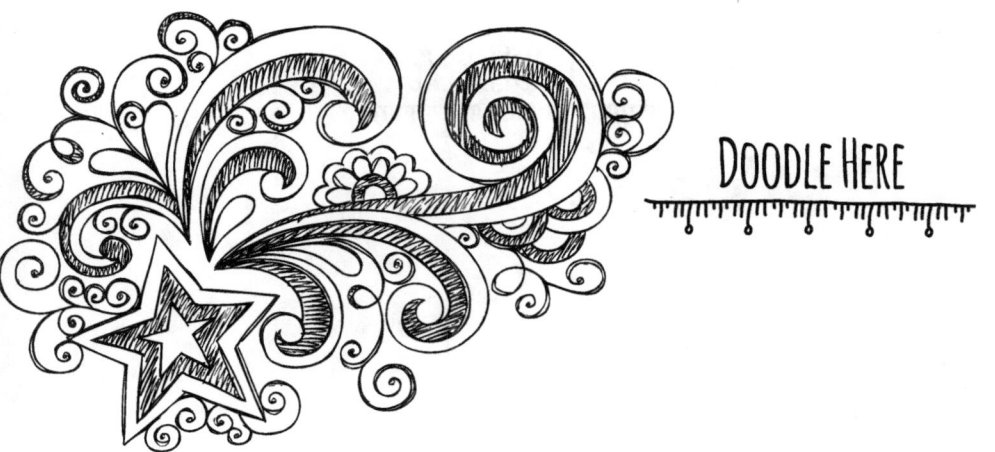

DOODLE HERE

DOODLE HERE

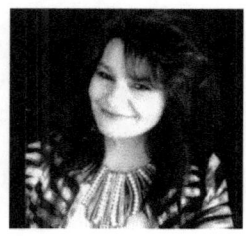

Cristie Will, BBA, CHC, CIC
Author

Cristie Will – An Accountant who traded in her calculator to master her calling to help people lose weight the healthy way and to gain optimal health and wellness.

Cristie found out how therapeutic doodling and coloring are for relaxation and creativity are by working with clients introducing coloring and doodling for stress relief. Discovering coloring and doodling she went on to create many books to help others relax, destress with joy.

Cristie lives in Johnstown, Colorado She has two grown children Lauren and Josh and four grandchildren.

Cristie received her training as a Certified Health Coach from the Institute for Integrative Nutrition training and training for her Cleansing Intensive Certification as a Cleansing Detoxing Coach from the Wild Rose College under Dr. Terry Willard CIH, PHD.

www.ingramcontent.com/pod-product-compliance
Lightning Source LLC
Chambersburg PA
CBHW070030210526
45170CB00012B/522